# Fire in the Hole!

*An Oral History of Moonshine and Murder
in Cumberland County, Kentucky*

# FIRE
## in the Hole!

An Oral History of
Moonshine and Murder
in Cumberland County,
Kentucky

Compiled and Edited by
Billy N. Guffey

ISBN 978-0-9797713-0-9
Library of Congress Control Number: 2007932942


Published by:
Xerxes Publishing
P.O. Box 785
Burkesville, KY 42717-0785
http://www.xerxespublishing.com
e-mail: info@xerxespublishing.com


1.0

# Contents

# Introduction

This book is the beginning of a much larger work, which is derived from oral interviews that were recorded as part of the Bicentenial Oral History Project. The project was headed by Jewell Thomas of the Lake Cumberland Library District in the 1970's and early 1980's.

Most of the interviews were conducted in the home of the informants, while others in the Cumberland County Library. The reader will find the term "informant" throughout the book, which refers to the person being interviewed, unless otherwise noted. All the informants agreed to the terms of the interview in writing, which states that permission is given for the conversation to be used in printed form. A full section of footnotes can be found at the back of this book. They, in turn, correspond to the footnote numbers placed throughout the text, and detail the informants name, the name of the interviewer, the place, date, and related information concerning the interview itself.

The process used to glean the information included in this book is simple yet labor intensive. The transcripts of the interviews were researched and indexed as to subject. These subjects were then assembled into a group of sections. This book is part of an ongoing project to assemble a much larger volume that will include chapters on Transportation, i.e. rafts, steamboats, horse and automobile; Crafts; Food; Communities; etc.

Fire in the Hole! has been printed as a small book in the hopes of receiving feedback as to whether a more complete, more encompassing, oral history book would be well received, and help determine the printing particulars of that future endeavour.

The book you are holding in your hands contains many stories concerning the craft of moonshining in Cumberland County; and also touches on a few instances of murder and other crimes. It must be noted here that no effort has gone into corroborating the information contained herein. This is a book of stories told by those in our community that had something to say. Oral history is very interesting in the ways that it is collected. Different people have different recollections of the same event from different viewpoints. Conflicting accounts of identical situations are not uncommon. It doesn't mean that one person is wrong, or fudging, in their facts, it simply means that they perceived things differently.

It should also be noted that every effort has been taken to record these stories in their true dialect, in a phonetic fashion. Such as using the word, "thar", instead of the correct spelling and pronunciation, "there". There is also the issue of language that needs to be mentioned here. While there is no inherent use of profanity in this book, there are a few instances of off-color language. I could say mild, but what might be mild to one person, could be harsh to another. There are also racial issues in some of the stories, with the "N"-word mentioned. As the editor of this compilation of stories I have agonized over the inclusion of this word, and whether to delete or replace it. But after consultations with those in the oral history field I feel it is important to leave the words as the informant stated them. Otherwise we tranform an incredible medium, the oral history, into hardly much more than a work of fiction.

The importance of oral history interviews to preserve our past is no small aspect of the recording of our history as a people. Many of the stories have not been heard by anyone other than immediate family members of those being interviewed. Thus, there is a virtual treasure of folklore and information that needs to be saved and made available to the general public.

The goal of this book is to take the verbal information, the memories, and organize them into an interesting format that is not only pleasing to read, but valuable for the study of folklore and rural life in this part of the Appalachian region.

The overall purpose of the book is to bridge the generational local history gap that seems to widen with the passing years. We must make sure that these stories are passed down to the next generation; whether it be on a front porch, or in the classroom.

I have attempted to keep my contributions to a minimum, and let the storytellers do the talking. There is, however, a need for introductions, brief histories, or lead-ins, due to the fact that the original interviews were conducted in question and answer format.

My hope is that the reader will find these stories entertaining, if not educational; not take anything contained in the tales too seriously; and enjoy a brief step back into a not too distant time and place, right here in our own backyard.

Billy N. Guffey, June, 2007

# Fire in the Hole!

*"It smells like gangrene starting in a mildewed silo; it tastes like the wrath to come; and when you absorb a deep swig of it you have all the sensations of having swallowed a lighted kerosene lamp. A sudden jolt of it has been known to stop a victim's watch, snap both of his suspenders, and crack his glass eye right across -- all in the same motion."*
*Irvin S. Cobb, Kentucky humorist*

Making homemade liquor is a craft that's been passed down in this region of Appalachia for many generations. When times were tough, the folks that lived in very rural areas depended on the income from the whiskey they made to feed their families. Cumberland County was no exception when it came to having its share of moonshiners. The deeply forested ridges and hollows of this area harbor an unlimited opportunity for hiding a still. For some it was an everyday occurance to make, drink, or sell it. Almost everyone knew about the trade.

> There were a lot of moonshiners back then. Back in them days. But I don't remember about who they were. But I know there were some. [1]

When asked about moonshiners that might have been set up near the Informant's former home on Ferris Fork, Cumberland County, he replied:

I don't know about that. All back this way to-
ward Mud Camp there were several they said. I
never did see one.

They had trouble, they caught a bunch one
night, back on Leatherwood, moonshining. That
what's they call moonshining... I think they tore
it down.[2]

Though making liquor might not have been one of the
most upstanding careers to undertake, it was one in which a
man could be proud if he had done it correctly. But, just as in
any job, the pride you take in performing your duties to the
best of your abilities, and producing a good product, is only
secondary when it comes at a price of guilt or shame.

I've bootlegged a little. I never did gamble. I
won't gamble. Yes, I made whiskey, get makers. We just put up a still, and just got us a plate
stand, set our worm down in it.

A worm is a crooked pipe you know. It's curled
around like this. And just sit down in it, it had
to be in there before you made whiskey, it's a
little spout that's coming out like a plate standing. There's corn and there's mash, and sweeten'
and all that in the still. And it just started boiling
and that steam is what makes the whiskey come
up at the elbow. Runs from the still to the plates
down where the worm was. Runs into that and a
round that and down in there. You set a bucket
down here and fruit jar under to catch it and a

stream just about the size of, maybe a little bigger, than a knitting needle, but not much bigger.

I remember one night we worked all night in dark. Just before day light we came out water bucket full, that's all we got.

Well back then it, I believe it was a dollar and half a pint, I believe it was back then. Or maybe a dollar and half a gallon. I guess that's what it was. That's weird ain't it?

The biggest thing is, probably the person is ashame of, but the bible saids nothing hide...will probably come out in light. What's the use of me trying to deny it...what I've done? I'm glad to be forgiven for it. I regret it.[3]

An unidentified source from Peytonsburg, Kentucky, now a reformed moonshiner who has since been saved "...by the Lord and I've been a worker ever since", speaks of revenuer, Big Six Henderson:

I was moonshining one time, and him and Stanley Groce come up on me. They caught me. I was carrying water. I looked up over the hill, I stepped over to get me a bucket of water out of the tub, that's what I had the water runnin' in, and I looked up; I aimed to take me some medicine, had asthma pretty bad at that time; I looked up, why I seed 'em. One of them hollered

15

at me. Walked back up to the place, it was all I could do to walk back up. I was caught before by another man. Big Six, though, he was the last 'un.

After I went up and got my time, and stayed about five months, six months, and got my parole, come back and, of course, they had a beer tax against me. Seventeen years from that time, why they had a $750 fine against me. That was seventeen years ago.

No, I never drank a drop since then. Never drunk a drop since. I drunk some before I was tried. But I never drunk none since I was tried. I drunk some the day before. The ninth day of November, 1954. Never drunk another drop since. Yeah, it'll be twenty years in April since I got out of prison, the first day of April.[4]

This same Informant gave the following response when questioned about why he decided to go into the moonshine business:

Oh, that time we just growed up. Our forefathers, my Dad he made it. And drunk it. And most of the people on the ridge made it. I think that more so than anything else. That's how. It's just handed on down.

Well, I learned a lot in Pennsylvania. That's why

16

I'd like to go back. I don't know. Other people had the experience I had. But I was sittin' there one night late; I'd made parole. He come and spoke to me. Said, "You know you're gonna leave here first day of April. If you were in hell, you'd never get out." And I think that woke me up. Well, I know it did. I wrote just a few lines home. And I told my woman, if I ever get home, I won't come back. I got home I guess the second day of April. There's a little church down there. Why, the Lord saved me and I've been a worker ever since. I only have one regret. That I didn't do it a long time ago.[5]

According to the interviewer, Informant A, of the previous story wept, and kept repeating, "The Lord saved me."

Moonshine also played a part in some of the dances that were held in the county back before the Second World War. "Turner Holler back over yander towards Marrowbone" and "over at Allen Creek" were two of the places the following Informant mentioned dancing and drinking taking place.

They done a lot of drinking at them. That's where their moonshine came in handy, that picked their spirit up.

When asked who called the set (the verbal 'call' for the square dance being performed), she replied;

Oh, Marsh Bryant...just first one then another. Marsh usually did. He get about half high and we'd be havin' fun. He'd be pitiful though. Course they'd drink a lot back then. About everytime you went to a party somebody had to be took home, so drunk he couldn't stand up.

Not too shy to mention some of the moonshiners of the time, or what she knew about the craft, she continued;

Oh Lord, Bill Branham was one of 'em. But you know, come to think of it, they's a whole lot of... whole bunch of 'em back then. Course they're still moonshiners but they nothing like they was back then. Whiskey, you couldn't go out no where and buy it. You had to make it, or some of the stills around. I know daddy used to take our molasses, have 'em made up into whiskey. This Branham back in the Branham Hollow (would do it).

I never did see one of 'em working. But that's the way they made it and they had these big tanks and then they had a worm that went around just like a bedspring. You've seen these old time bedsprings they have that go around, that's the way they'd go. Just like a bee hive or something. Only it would be just a little round thing where's this bee hive, you know, would be kindly lagged off a little.

He's the only one that I really knowed.

*FIRE IN THE HOLE!*

It wudn't against the law back then. Well, course it could have been against the law though, I don't know, they made it anyway. So, I don't reckon they's afraid of being caught. If they was they didn't show it.

Just took 'em more whiskey and sugar, or more corn and sugar, to make it out of. Or they'd take meal. Course that's what they'd call making the mash out of the meal. And then they put in the still and run it through there.

Lord, I don't know (the cost to make it), it wudn't that expensive back then. It had corn, water, yeast in it. It's stuff you put in there to sour it. I don't remember whether it was in cakes then or just in the powder. That (the time to make moonshine) I don't know. I know daddy wudn't have his molasses over there too long till they have the bottles filled and back over at the barn. They wudn't take it to the house they'd take it to the barn... Keep the children from getting it. The children back then, shoot, they drank just about as bad as men did if they didn't keep it hid from 'em. Well, they loved the taste of it. Yeah... Shoot I wudn't give a half a pint of moonshine for a gallon of this other stuff they bring in.

Well, now I've heard of some who's bought it, but I don't know where they bought it at.[6]

Inevitably, when talk turns to moonshining, the stories of

19

revenuers are not far behind. Mr. Carlas Pitcock was a store owner and farmer in the Mud Camp Community of Cumberland County. The story he relates took place near Centerpoint which is just across the Cumberland River in Monroe County, and speaks to the lengths a revenue man would go to get his man. Certainly a trait most of the federal men shared.

There was some moonshiners. I'll tell you about them. I don't care. It's all done past anyway. Dave White was one, Martin Vibbert was one and they was several more. Then, was the ones made on my dad's place you know. And they was some more close around, you know. Billy Brown, and a Luke Jones and Garrett Jones, Wes Crawford and several more too numerous to mention.

They sold it in pints, and quarts and half gallons and gallons. Back then a gallon, got to be about 10 dollars. Course when we first started it was cheaper that. Maybe four dollars a gallon at first you know. It got up to about ten.

Some got caught by the revenuers. Yeah, some did. Dewey Head over there in Centerpoint he got caught by a revenue man. He (the revenue man) dressed up in old clothes. Come down there and got with his brother. He had a brother drank pretty heavy. He thought it was just a tramp come through you know. Dressed in old shotty clothes. So he got him to go with him. He said he wanted to know where he could get him some whiskey. He took him, you know, to his brothers. Where he made you know. And got the whiskey so he went back to town. He got the sheriff, you know. Come down there and captured him. I don't remember his name.[7]

When asked if he ever raided a moonshine still, the following Informant, Mr. Will Jones, former Cumberland County Sheriff (1913-1917), proceeded to tell the following story regarding his hunt for a still and the reaction from the local population of the area where the liquor was discovered; and also the reaction of those people in Burkesville who liked a little sip every now and then, and had heard about the raid.

I raided several moonshine stills. I never did catch anybody with them; but one Saturday, about dinner, E.G. McFarland, a revenue man, called me from Albany to meet him at the Milt Smith place (he lived out there on the ridge between Kettle and Modoc), about sun down, and to bring somebody with me. My deputy was done gone and wasn't in town. Ham Garner was deputy jailer and I got him to go with me and we got out there at Milt Smith's about sun down.

They were eatin' supper out there and we hadn't had no supper. They was in a hurry to get started, and we went on and we walked them hills and hollers out there at Red Banks and Kettle Creek all night and on up to dinner the next day. And I still hadn't got nothing to eat since at dinner the day before.

21

We found a little still down there in the holler, pretty close to old Uncle Claude Riley and cut it up and never found no liquor, but they had run it once; had a big lot of backing, they called it, and the next time they run it, that made the liquor. We poured them out and cut the still up and come up there to old Uncle Claude Riley's. eleven o'clock I guess when we got there.

Uncle Claude's wife was named Betty. There was five of us, and I asked Aunt Betty, "Would you fix dinner for us, fine?" She said she would and she turned in to getting our dinner. Mr. McFarland got out in the garden prowling around, and I went with him. He said, "There is liquor buried here in this garden somewhere."

We found a ten-gallon keg full of liquor, a three- or four-gallon churn full, buried down and had a cloth tied over the top of the churn. The keg was buried by the churn and we dug that up and brought it in the back yard.

While Aunt Betty was getting dinner, I guess forty or fifty neighbors come in. They knew we were in the neighborhood. A revenue man could go down there and it would spread like wildfire, and everybody knowed it in no time. I guess there was forty or fifty there by the time she got dinner ready, and they put a dipper in that churn of liquor, and everybody that come would drink out of the dipper. And, I seen they were going to drink it all up. I asked Aunt Betty if she had a bottle handy, and she said she had a fruit jar, and I got a half-gallon fruit jar full of that liquor.

By the time we eat dinner and got back out there, there wasn't a bit of liquor in that churn. I asked Mr. McFarland, "What are you going to do with this liquor, this keg?" And he said, "Knock the head out of it." I looked around and found a crooked piece of iron was there, 4 or 5 feet long, and I knocked the head out of the keg and it was on a bank right above the spring. It run right over in the spring.

While we was eating dinner, I seen the boys going backward and forward through the kitchen getting buckets and things, but I didn't think nothing. They said they had stole every bit of that keg of liquor, and filled that keg full of water. Of course, it run over in the spring. Afterward, they told me themselves, they had stole every bit of that liquor.

Anyway, I got my half-gallon jar full back to town. Peyton Smith and Jessie married that evening, and I aimed to go to Louisville with them, but we never got away down there until after twelve. I got up there at Dad's, I guess, two o'clock and set my jar of liquor up on the mantle.

23

Old Captain Strange, who lived just across the street from us, come over there, come a hopping across the street. He had a cancer on his lip, and he asked me did I bring any of that liquor home. The news had done got back to town that we had found it. I don't know how it had spread like it did, telephone, I reckon. He come on in and told Mama to give him a glass, and Mama gave him a glass. He got him a glass full and drank it and went back over and set down on the porch.

By the time I had got dressed to go to Louisville, he had come back for more. He come back and got him another glass full. Old Jess Coe and every old man in town was there and when I left, about three o'clock anyway, it wasn't an inch deep in that half-gallon fruit jar. Every old man in town had to have a drink of that liquor.[8]

Here the interviewer asked if Mr. Jones had to use the whiskey for evidence, to which he stated, "No." And then acknowledged that it was of good quality, saying, "Yes, the best there was."[9]

It is important at this point in the narration to explain a little about about the Coe Ridge colony that figures so prominently in the stories to come. There is an area in the southern part of Cumberland County called Coe Ridge, which is a spur of a larger land formation known as Pea Ridge. Virtually inaccessable in the busy days of moonshining, there was one good road that lead down over the ridge, and in those days, calling it a road was most likely a stretch of the term.

The story of Coe Ridge was brought to the general public's attention with the publication of Dr. William Lynwood Montell's book, The Saga of Coe Ridge - A Study in Oral History. For a much more complete history of the community, please refer to Dr. Montell's book. Although, for the sake of clarification in this work, the author will make the reader aware that the Coe Colony was an entity unto itself. Founded by freed slaves, the community was isolated from the outside world, which in turn, lead to many problems within the colony. Because of the isolation, inhabitants suffered from economic hardships, and along with the state of the land on which they lived, this left very few options for making money and supporting their families. This, combined with other factors, eventually lead to the mass migration of the families that had lived there for almost a hundred years.

One of the few ways for the population of Coe Ridge to support themselves was by doing what they knew best. And that was making moonshine.

A local country store owner, Keith Brewington, was asked about any problems with moonshiners that he remembered:

> Back five or six years ago or maybe further back, I recall they had a lot of moonshining up on Coe Ridge. They had a lot of moonshining and they would make moonshine, and people would buy it and they'd feel happy after they drunk it, so we

25

don't have any of that any more.

Everybody is quit, I mean they have taverns and beer joints and things that's handy to get, so they've all quit this hard way. But back then you could get a gallon of liquor for a dollar. Now it's about twenty dollars a gallon, I think. You see how its jumped, real corn liquor has, and back at that time it was really pure corn liquor. It wouldn't no imitation or nothing, it was real stuff, and it didn't hurt you like lot of this they have anymore. I mean it. It's better.

They used it more for medicine, seem like, the old people did. Then, sometimes, they would have the colic pretty often and get to drinking it, but it would kinda help them on the side.[10]

By 1904 the Coes on the Ridge were known to be making and selling whiskey. Bill Poindexter tells of buying moonshine from Calvin Coe:

I used to go through thar and buy whiskey from them back when I was young. I'd go through thar and buy whiskey from them. Me and Oss Coffey was coming from Arat, up from Leslie, with a drove of hogs the first time I ever bought any whiskey from them. And it was a-poring down the rain on us.

And I seen Old Uncle Cal a-coming. I told Oss, "If he's got any whiskey, I'll get me a pint of

*FIRE IN THE HOLE!*

whiskey from him." He rode up and I asked him, and he said, "Yessir, I've got it."

Well, that hope us up.[11]

One story that has passed down in different forms concerns the teaching of the moonshining craft to the young people of the colony. A few different versions follow:

> One time when Judge Wells was running for judge, he was campaigning on the ridge for the Nigger vote. He went back to the school, and before he walked in the school he could hear E Coe saying, "Now, yesterday we studied the making of the mash, and tomorrow we will study how to run off a batch."
>
> Old Man E Coe seen that Judge Wells saw the diagram on the board and had overheard. So E knew that he better help Wells out. Every Nigger on the ridge voted for Wells due to E Coe's influence.[12]

Montell also relates in a footnote on the same page that "Royce Cary told the tale in more authentic tones; in his account, it was claimed that Old Man E had a model still in the schoolhouse, and that he would constantly write the whiskey-making recipe on the blackboard until the children could recite it from memory.[13]

The Cumberland County News quotes Joe Creason of the Louisville Courier Journal magazine (Nov. 1957) as stating

27

that Big Six Henderson told the story of how he had hid "once under the rear of the Coe Ridge School while classes were in progress. Finally, the teacher, a ridge resident, dismissed school for the day. "Now, chillun," he told them as they left, "tomorrer we is goin' to take up mixin' in the mash."[14]

William Bernard (Big Six) Henderson is probably the most well-known revenuer to have ever worked this area of Appalachia. He "participated in the seizure of more than 5,000 stills in the 28 years he was a federal agent."[15] In 1954 or 1955, Big Six and his agents confiscated 224 stills; however, ten years later "we went for months without catching a still, hearing word of one. That's how much it slacked off."[16] Big Six found a total of 304 moonshine stills in Cumberland County. This is more captures than any other county in Kentucky in twenty-five years.[17] The stories of Big Six are still told by those old enough to remember the lawman and his never-ending struggle to stop moonshining in the region. And, of course, Big Six wasn't alone in his quest. Many other law enforcement agents acted as revenuers. Quinn Pearl was another moonshine chaser that worked the hills and hollers, along with Isom Williams, Charley Summers, Mark Holmes, and Elmer Davis, just to name a few from the federal jurisdiction; and many local officials through the many decades of hunting stills and the makers.

> There's a settlement over here called Coe Ridge.
> It's close to the Kentucky-Tennessee line where
> a group of people came in after slavery. They
> were part Indian and part black. A couple of
> white women came in there in later years and
> took up with them, and they were a mixture of

*FIRE IN THE HOLE!*

white, black, and Indian. Their profession was making moonshine whiskey.

My first trip over there was on 12 March 1942. We caught seven moonshine stills that day and destroyed about three hundred gallons of illicit whiskey. So it fascinated me to catch these fellows. And, in twenty-three or twenty-four years I was here, I caught practically everyone over there that could walk or run or crawl. But I didn't mistreat them and it became a game with me. And I go back over there now and I see a few of them that I sent to the penitentiary. They'll holler at me cause I treated them like I wanted to be treated. And the men knew it. The gun play was out over there. When I first went in, we had a lot of shooting and all after Prohibition. I think they finally found out that you can't win against the federal government.

We had an unwritten law. A man by the name of Isom Williams was a former school teacher in Monroe County, Kentucky. He told me when I came here, 'Big Six, you won't find it in any memorandum or any orders from Washington, D.C., but we have an unwritten law where if anyone shoots you or kills you, I'll never take 'em in. I'm gonna ask you the same request.' So that was my Bible the twenty-eight years I was in there - that I would never take one moonshiner in that deliberately killed a man performing his duty.[18]

*FIRE IN THE HOLE!*

In the latter years of moonshining in Cumberland County it would appear on the surface that the moonshiners and the revenuers got along better than could be expected, especially with the potential outcome taken into consideration.

> "I really came to respect the moonshiners I chased," Henderson says. "When I broke in, William H. Kinnaird, then in charge of the Louisville office, gave me some advice I never forgot. 'You're going to be arresting people who often can't read or write,' he said. 'But if you give them credit for having at least 10 percent more brains than you do, you'll get along.'"[19]

Even though the most violent period of the Ridge had passed by the time Henderson came onto the scene, the resentment between the two sides would always be there.

The stories of Big Six Henderson and the Coe Ridge Colony are infamous in this part of the country. Henderson played a large role in the final demise of this proud rural black community that sat upon a rough, nearly inaccessible ridge. Whether it was his intention to do so is a question that will never be answered. But the real-life stories in which he took part will always live in the memories of those who are old enough to remember, and through the stories printed here.

> One time back when Big Six was workin' this area he was out on the Ridge (Coe Ridge). Well, these two men had a still. Their names were

*FIRE IN THE HOLE!*

Homer Spears and Press Scott. This real old fella, Jim Shack Short, came walkin' down this holler with two ears of corn in his pocket. Well, Big Six had to take them all to Bowling Green for court. Jim kept tellin' Big Six that he was out there lookin' for his cow, but Big Six said he'd still have to go to court. Well, the judge let him off cause he was an old man, but Big Six told him to keep his damn cow at home.[20]

Henderson is known to have gone to extreme lengths to get his man in the act of making moonshine. Many times the revenuers would hide in areas where the still was in view and wait for the moonshiner to run off a batch before they made their raid.

Once Henderson allowed himself to be covered over with leaves not more than ten feet from the still pot. He lay there most of the night. About 8 a.m. three men appeared, built a fire under the pot and began to work.

"Man alive," one of the men joked to the others as they ran off the first batch, "wouldn't ol' Big Six Henderson like to see me now." The man almost died of fright when, no sooner had he gotten the words out of his mouth, Henderson grabbed him by the ankles.[21]

Fuzz Anders, a resident of Coe Ridge, was always a challenge for Big Six. They seemed to have an understanding that

31

they both were at the height of their respective games, and the end result, the worm you might say, could turn for either. Fuzz was a large, light complected black man that stood about six foot three inches in his bare feet. Which is how you would have to measure him since he hardly ever wore shoes. He did wear shoes when he ventured into town, but claimed he didn't like them, they hurt his feet. He had long, curly, unkempt hair and beard and piercing blue eyes. He hardly ever left the ridge, even in his later years. He lived in a small shack by himself, with a wood cookstove placed outside under a tree in the summer, on the same ridge that he called home all his life. When everyone else had gone. Fuzzy stayed.

Henderson recalls one meeting with Anders:

> I was over there with Williams and couple of deputies one morning and we found this still just about daylight. So Williams and I got up on the hill and we were gonna come down. It was on a ravine where we could run almost into a chute. And we had Sheriff Brown and a couple of his deputies with us. Williams and I were gonna divide up and come down the ridge on 'em and slip up and catch 'em.

> So it was about...just a few minutes after daylight. And about thirty minutes, here comes these three black boys down to the still. And they were about twenty, twenty-two years old...youngsters and makin' a lot of noise.

And so they went to work about setting up the still. And we had been there about twenty or thirty minutes when we looked up and here came this old boy with a white beard about two or three inches. And he had a cane, a crutch, takin' his time comin' down from the ridge. He spent fifteen, twenty minutes workin' his way down.

Williams was right there beside me and he nudged me and said, "I'll catch him." I said, "You would pick on a cripple." So we waited till he got down and he sat down on around the still. So we started slippin' down to the still. We divided and I started about halfway down there and this old boy looked up and saw us. And he let out a yell and dropped that crutch and took off. We caught the other three. He's the only one that got away from us. That was old Fuzzy...We picked him up a short time later. [22]

The previous story was told by Big Six Henderson in 1973. Fuzzy Anders was interviewed in 1979 and related his version of the same incident.

Big Six run me off way down in this holler down here one time. I was walkin' on crutches, had my leg cut in two. I was walkin' on crutches. Me and another boy went down in thar, Joe Coe was a makin' down in that holler.

We went down thar to get us a drink, and we got

33

*FIRE IN THE HOLE!*

down in thar, and they was a big bluff of rock thar. Says, "Joe" says, "that's a helluva bluff thar for a man to have to climb ain't it." He said, "I'll have to climb it anytime." Said, "I seen some strange tracks in here this mornin'." And we didn't pay much attention to it.

I laid over on my crutches and shove...up under the furnace, to get a start you know, to get me a shot. All at once Joe Coe said, "Look out boys! Thar they come!" and I throwed them crutches away, Big Six took out after me and I just slided out from under him just like that. Run off and left him. I got on top of the hill back in old man E's field back thar. Wudn't enough my leg was cut in two, it was just a throbbin' you know, like that? And I sat down on some logs thar. All at once a big rabbit jumped out from under thar, out from them logs, I thought it was one of them after me, I got up and took off again. I come back down Ray's, he lived down below where I live now, and I went down thar and Ray's old lady come to the door, said "What's wrong?" I said, "The revenues et." I got out and went on around the ridge, and directly here come Howard Short an Big Six.

I seen 'em comin' down the road...A big hickora tree thar and I laid down upon the hickora tree thar with some sprouts out thar, and I laid down so they couldn't see me. Big Six come on thar, told Howard Short, "I'm gonna take a picture

34

*FIRE IN THE HOLE!*

of old man Robert's house." And he took a picture of old man Robert's house and went on out the ridge and askin' about me. "Well, if you see Fuzz, tell him to come on down Bowling Green and make bond in the morning." Well, I got old man Cal, uncle Robert, and old man Will Dowel lives on kettle creek, a white guy.

I went down thar to make my bond, and we went in Big Six's office, and Big Six, he was talkin' to me thar. Showin' me the picture takin' of old man Robert's house, them hickory trees thar. And I said, "Big Six, you look pretty close down in thar," I said, "you'll see me in thar." He looked and I had my head stickin' up. He said, "Well Fuzz, that is you thar ain't it?" "Yeah," I said, "I could have reached out and got you by the britches leg."[23]

Humorous though these stories may be, there is always the fact that if the perpetrator is caught, he will most likely go to prison. There is also a definite ring of truth in these two versions of the same story. And very interesting. Henderson telling his story in 1973, and Fuzz relating his in 1979. Emmit Cain was also quoted in The Saga of Coe Ridge as saying,

"Anders had his leg cut off nearly. And he was jist a-flyin'; run off and left his crutches. And Henderson found his crutches. He took them up and throwed them down in his brother's yard and told him to give Anders his crutches when he come in."[24]

35

Although Elbert "Fuzz" Anders is mentioned in several stories alongside Henderson, and they both, at times, showed mutual respect, it was also a potentially threatening situation each time these two met. Which made for ill tempers and nervous reactions from both sides at times.

One of the times I caught Fuzzy Anders I knew I was in for him... He was in there mixin' up the mash. He had it in a box. They had no barrels, but they made their own boxes from lumber. The hardest thing to drive a nail into and the hardest thing to tear up...But they made and had a big 200-gallon box to ferment mash.

I went over there, and he was over there inside with his overalls. And he had his pants rolled up, and about size twelve or thirteen foot. And these other two Negroes, Van Coe was one of them, and, the other one was Homer, I believe.

Anyway they was carrying the water and mixin' the mash. He's in there mixin' it with his feet, while they were pourin' it in. He was jumpin' around there. I went up and caught him before he could get out of the box. If he got out of the box, he would probably give you a hell of a run. And he might get away from you. But he didn't think that was fair. He cried about halfway, "Mr. Henderson, you cheated me! That wasn't fair." I said, "What do you mean? I'm just here to arrest you. Wasn't any question of playing games with you." But he thought I should let him get out and take off, I guess.[25]

When Fuzz was asked "what kind of fella" Big Six was, he stated,

> Well. When Big Six first come in this country, he was a nice man. And the longer he come in here, the worse he got.[26]

Former Cumberland County Sheriff Maurice Clifton "Doc" Keen, mentions the foot chases that the revenuers engaged in with the moonshiners. It should be remembered that in the era in which this took place, walking was the mode of transportation for a large portion of the population, especially on Coe Ridge, where even a horse to ride was considered a luxury. So it is not a surprise that the men being chased, along with those in pursuit, would become quite adept at running, and would have made any track coach envious of their talent.

> There were a lot of moonshiners out on the ridge, Coe Ridge. This one fella, Fuzzy Anders, used to give Six hell. Fuzz always had a still a goin'. He never wore shoes so when Six would go out to catch him, Fuzz would run like hell. One time Six had to run him, I know, two miles to catch him.[27]

Speaking of the foot chase, Fuzz Anders stated:

> Big Six never did catch me. He said he was gonna catch me, but he never did. I never have been

37

caught. I run off and they swear to me...I was always too fast on my feet for 'em.[28]

Big Six Henderson was quoted in the Cumberland County News...

Track coaches brag about the four minute mile, but in the old days, there were a dozen men on Coe Ridge who could break it.[29]

Sheriff J.B. Groce was known to have chased many moonshiners through the woods during his term. Emmit Cain related a tale of Sheriff Groce outrunning a moonshiner one time:

They run this colored boy out thar one time. And they wuz a big fence up and they's a hog hole under the fence. Man Groce wuz with Big Six. And the boy said he knowed Man Groce wuz a-going to catch. Said he run him full blast down hill. And said he fell, and said he hit that hog hole just a-center. Said Man Groce wuz on the other side of the fence and ready to grab hold of him.[30]

Once a man was caught he usually ended up in court in Bowling Green. It would seem that some were considerably slower on their feet than others, as can be attested to by the following story...

Joe Coe was one of the leaders over there (on Coe Ridge), I caught him so many times and

*FIRE IN THE HOLE!*

brought him down here (Bowling Green, KY). I think Judge Milliken was the judge that was trying to represent him in court. So judge asked him, he said, "Joe, what kind of record do you have?" He said, "Judge, my record is pafect." He said, "What do you mean 'pafect'?" He said, "I been down here eight times, and they sent me to the penitentiary eight times."[31]

Joe Coe was another resident of the Ridge that had many dealings with the law. Sometimes it went in the lawman's favor, and other times to the moonshiners.

One time he had a team (of mules) down there (Coe Ridge). I slipped down on him one day and he was comin' up here and he had a wagon. I was expecting to see a still over there. And...he had this flat bed wagon with a couple of mules drivin' up there, and I come out on him. I said, "What you got there, Joe?" He said, "Got some water." And I thought it was moonshine cause it...I checked the jugs. It was water. I thought sure I had him with about twenty- or thirty-gallons of moonshine. I thought maybe he was pullin' a trick on me, had part of 'em whiskey and part of 'em water. But they were all water. Haulin' water up to the house.[32]

Warning systems have always been employed in one form or another to protect one's property, safety and livelihood; and even though the men making whiskey were in some of the most remote areas of the county, it was still possible to warn others of impending danger, even from the depth of the woods.

> ...the Coe Negroes developed a warning system as a means of notifying each other when the law was at hand. The first of the moonshiners to see an officer would throw back his head and yell, "Fi-i-i-re in the hole." The yell was strangely like a yodel in which the long vowels were accented. The last syllable was long and was held on a high note. Like an echo, the yell was repeated by another still farther along the ridge, then another, and so on until the call had reached the deepest ravine occupied by a moonshine still.[33]

Another example of this same warning system being used:

> We'd located this still and I was gonna wait till these two Coe Ridge boys, Davis Marshal Anders and Ernest Anders were comin'. We waited there. They had hung their jackets up on a tree limb, over there on the side of the still...had gone to lunch. They'd been down there just gettin' everything set up to make. So we came in and located. I'd already found them several days before.
>
> They came down the path and was down on the other side. I was just waitin'. I motioned for the

other two officers to remain quiet. I was waitin' for their arrival at the still site when I heard this voice. I didn't see him, but I heard this voice. I heard him holler, "Fire in the hole!" And when he did, they stopped, you know. And I knew they were gonna take off. So I jumped up and started runnin' them. Run them right back up the path. And when they did, this Anders, he gave out. He just slid down. I saw who he was. And kept after Davis Marshal. But anyway he ran right around his house. He didn't even stop. He didn't go in the house, he kept on runnin'. We were right beside of him. I run him on down there and finally he dropped before I did. He looked up and said, "Mr. Henderson, I'm not gonna run." I said, "I know damn well you're not! Cause I'm gonna hold on to you." So I got him by the belt and marched him right on back down to the still. I didn't turn loose of him. But he was about seventeen years old. I tell you, that boy could blow the dust![34]

In the Elbert Anders interview he demonstrated the yell, "Fire in the Hole!" and stated that when this was heard "they scatter just like the bees."[35]

According to Royce Cary, the warning system was not limited to one type of call:

They used to have a noise they'd make 'fore the revenue'd get there. They'd have a man, have one of them kids spotted up on one of them trees out there. He'd be way up in one of them trees, you know. When he'd see the revenue, why, he'd make a noise through his mouth er blow through his hands -- make a noise. That'd give the others time to get back the stuff out of the way before he'd (i.e. revenue man) get there.[36]

Relating the story of a large raid on Coe Ridge that occurred on 27 January 1954, Big Six Henderson, along with other law officials captured seven stills. It just goes to show you, that all alarm systems are not foolproof. Big Six stated:

...in the raiding party were seven cars which carried revenue agents, local officials, and state policemen. It was prearranged that the lead car would stop at the first Negro house, the second car at the second house, and so on until all seven houses on the ridge were entered and searched. Seven arrests were made. Three offenders were sent to prison, while the other four were placed on probation on their promises to leave Kentucky. (Note here the promise to leave the state, which is also found in another story.) I got two undercover men and brought them in here (Coe Ridge). I brought them in after dark, and I went over on the ridge and pointed out the places where I knew they had reports. They were bootleggin' and foolin' with whiskey.

And...so we went on down to the lake and we went down to Holly Creek down in Tennes-

*FIRE IN THE HOLE!*

see. And I stayed down there. They were to go back in the night. So the next night they come on over there to make a buy. They pretend that they were fishermen down by the lake. One of them was a fellow from Bowling Green, and he had a red nose. He looked like one of these whiskey men anyway. A drunkard, you might say. The other fella, a little fella, was a agent out of Indianapolis. He didn't look like an officer and they don't even get questioned hardly. They told 'em that they were fishing down on the lake and they went over and they bought from everybody, nearly, over there. And we spent three or four days over there. I never will forget this one, Ollie Pruitt. Ollie was selling whiskey at the time. They went in, and, I think, it was five-gallons they bought from him. So they came on back and we finished up that week. We went on out to Bowling Green. We came back the next week and I told 'em to go over and get another buy. They went over and got another buy from Ollie there at the store. And it was right at the time this candle egg law came in, the federal government was involved in. You know, and eggs had to be candled before they were sold.

So there was this big egg crate settin' full of eggs. And Hendricks was the ABC fella from Bowling Green that I'd brought over here. And he wanted to take some eggs home with him. We were goin' back in a day or two. So he just told him, he said, "We've just about run out of eggs over there over to the lake. How about sellin' me a dozen or two of those eggs?" He said, "Oh hell, I can't sell you any of those eggs. If I sold you any of those eggs, Uncle Sam would throw me underneath the jail. Not in it!"

They went back the next night, Thursday night. They couldn't buy from anybody. And everybody was closed up tight. They didn't have any to sell. I wondered if anybody had given them the alarm or something. But I found out later that somebody had come down to Holly Creek Inn, and they saw my name on that register.

Stanley Groce and I got seven of 'em. Got Bully Wilburn and four others at one still. Then, we slipped over after we chased 'em and noise was made, we went back and, and they were working over at another still over at another hollow. And I sent Stanley over around the hill to come in on 'em and we got in on 'em, and we got Charlie and Ottlie Coe at that time. And we got Bully Wilburn and the whole bunch of 'em over at the other one still. We, the two of us, I think, end up, just the two of us, we had seven men. We had seven of 'em and two big stills and we must have had sixty-gallons of whiskey. That's the day Bully Wilburn, I was runnin' Bully Wilburn, and he turned his head around and lookin' right straight at me, and runnin' just straight the other way. He turned around and looked at me 'fore I ever caught him. I caught him. In fact, I got two of 'em up there. And there was a couple of 'em that got away we picked up. Of course, they all come in. They all pled guilty. There wasn't a question about every one of 'em.[37]

One informant was a moonshiner who seemed to think he was as smart as Big Six Henderson. He tells a story of beating Big Six and the law.

One time when Big Six was workin' this area I had a still back behind the house. I went down and checked it one day and then went over to my father's. Mann Groce and Big Six walked up to the house and set this gallon jug on the porch. I knew what it was. I hadn't been gone from the still but five minutes. I didn't know they was around.

"Well," Big Six said, "Do you know what this is?" I said, "No, can't say's I do." Big Six said, "Do you know whose it is?" I said, "I don't know who's damn jug it is." Big Six said, "Well, we'll take it to get fingerprints." Mann Groce reached down and picked it up. Well, I knew they couldn't take fingerprints after Mann'd picked it up.

A few weeks later, I got a summons from Bowling Green. I ignored it.

Later, I was over at my father's house and Big Six

45

said, "Informant B?" I said, "Yep, that's me." He said, "I've come to take you to Bowling Green." I said, "Well, can I go change my clothes?" He said, "Go ahead."

So I came up to the house and changed my clothes. He took me in and brought me back. A free ride to Bowling Green.[38]

The original interviewer states that a cousin of the informant was present during the interview and that both "seemed to enjoy the idea beating the law" and that the informant's attitude was "one of mockery" towards Big Six Henderson.

Another time Big Six stated that he received a telephone call from a woman in Burkesville concerning her son who seemed to have drank too much moonshine...

I had a woman call me from Burkesville over here one day at three o'clock. She's the woman that would call me. Her boy would get tight. I caught him at a damn still one time. She gave me the information on him, and I caught him down there drunk. Of course, he wadn't runnin' it. But he'd drink the drink all the time. She had a boy. And she'd set there, and they'd set there and talk about it, and she'd hear it, and, damn, she'd draw me a map. And she could imagine it, and that map would be just as accurate as anything you ever saw. A still in operation on top of Pea Ridge here. In two hours I left the office and

*FIRE IN THE HOLE!*

when we got over there they were sacking up the whiskey. They had fourteen-gallons run off and it was corn whiskey.[39]

Not only did Henderson and and the other law officials have to contend with trying to apprehend the moonshiners in the setting of the woods, they also had to worry about the men who transported the 'shine after it was made. Bootlegging has many definitions, one of which is, the transporting of alcoholic beverages in a dry county. One such bootlegger proved a challenge to Big Six over a period of time.

This bootlegger did it to me. He transported from Tennessee up here to Kentucky. He'd go to the used car spot down there below Livingston. I knew who he was. But he'd come in there after dark. And he'd drive a different car everytime he come in.

But I finally caught him. But it took me about six months to catch him. Cause we didn't know when he was coming. He'd pass me sometimes in the night. And I would be looking for the car he came in the last night. He had a different car. One night I laid over there till five o'clock in the morning. Gave up looking for him and an hour later he came in. I found him after it was too late. I finally caught on and I finally caught him. He was right over down close to the lake...below Celina. Horse Creek Camp, I believe was the name of it.[40]

*FIRE IN THE HOLE!*

Another meeting between Big Six Henderson and Joe Coe took place on the blacktop and not in the woods:

> Joe was haulin' whiskey to, out to Willie Porter Short, out there, I'd heard. I'd had that report. So I got over here early one morning and had Mann Groce with me, and, ah, one of the other agents. And we were gonna drive out there, out that road that leads off the highway, down there, to go on down to Coe Ridge, and catch 'em as they come out there. But we didn't get over there.
>
> Before we got there, I met Joe. And he saw me as he was comin' out. Well, I whipped around and started after him. And I turned the siren on and he was ignoring it. And I bumped into him. And he come to a halt pretty fast. And we got out and he said, "I haven't got anything."
>
> So we went back there and, of course, we found six gallons in the back. He'd gone on past Willie Porter Short's. He didn't stop. He was heading on down to Tennessee. We got this whiskey out of the back end and he had these corn cob stoppers in it, and the whiskey was still hot. And we knew he had just run it off. So I told Mann Groce to take Joe and take him on back to Burkesville and put him in jail. I'd pick him up later. We went on down there later, down below his house, and this still was still hot. There wasn't anybody around, but, of course, they didn't come in.[41]

*FIRE IN THE HOLE!*

When asked about a revenuer named Isom Williams, Elbert Anders said that he knew Williams for 30 years. And that "he got rough." Speaking of a time when one of the Coe Ridge resident's wife had just a day before given birth to a son; Isom Williams thought he had his man...

> Well, Bobby was born that day before that. And Sam got down on Judio, to get some castorie, you know, for his old lady, you know. And uh, Isom and them come in, when Sam come from the store, and Isom, he tore up from the holler...over in there, and Sam had done been down to the store and come back. He came in and told Sam, says "Sam," says, "Did you run off from that moonshine still over yonder wallago?" Sam said, "I ain't run off from no moonshine still." Says, "I just been down the store and got some medicine. Castorie, for my wife." He said, "No. That was you Sam." Isom said, "The baby just born yesterday evenin'." He said, "I'm gonna tell you one thing Sam, when you get back outta the pen, that little nigger baby will be white-headed." That's what he told Sam. Sam told 'im, said, "Maybe not." They took Sam on to Bowling Green, where he made bond, and went to be tried, and Sam told the judge what Isom Williams said. He told 'im. And the judge turned Sam loose.[42]

Violence was a normal occurance when you were in the business of moonshining, or attempting to apprehend those breaking the law. Many people were injured, or lost their lives in the pursuit of money through illegal activities during the period when moonshine ruled the ridges. Henderson raided one still with Keith Speck, a Kentucky State Trooper from Albany, and had this to say:

> We went over on the Ridge one time. Out at Grider Hill Dock. We had located and knew this still was over there. I slipped over there and found it. He (Keith Speck) let me out of the car and I found the still. Then, we started goin' back to it. The only way we could get up there without them seeing us was to go up there in a boat and come up in there. Go in the back and climb this bluff and get up over in there. Go in the back, the still without them seein' us come in. You know, we'd come in the back side.
>
> And while we was goin' over there there was this old goat that had turned wild...And we didn't bother him. We'd just get up every morning and go on over to the still. We carried that on for about three weeks.Try to find out where they were makin' it. A couple of times they would get in there and make it before we got there. Of course, you know, I had to come all the way from Bowling Green, and it was in the wintertime. And the water was so awful there, we'd go down to the dock manager, we knew him, this Sloanes boy, we knew he had something going on there. We didn't try to advertise it. We hid our guns under our raincoats, our heavy coats. We'd take our shoes off as soon as we'd get in

the boat. It was so rough, there wasn't anybody else on that lake but us. We were afraid it would capsize. We'd get up there and we'd have to go up the lake about two miles. Up to Piney Falls and climb that bluff. And we'd generally see that old goat up on the hill looking down on us.

We'd slip back in there and one day I slipped in there to check it. Keith had let me out of the car and went on up there. And I saw these two fellas and they were up there putting thread over the path, black thread so they could find out if we'd came in, see. I was waiting for them to go in and stir up the ashes. They never did. They went down to the still but they never did make any move when I could pick them up. For when Keith came back, we still had to go back later and pick them up in the still, at the still. One of them (was killed by Speck). And, of course, I'd caught this other bird. I'd pulled him out a couple of times and threatened to kill him. But fortunately I didn't have to. But Keith had killed his brother and he'd tried to kill Keith. Or, we thought he did. So I, I told Keith not to kill him unless we had to. But we kept going over there. And we got in there one morning before daylight, a little before. And sure enough, little while later he came in, he and this other fellow, came on down to the still. So we caught them. So I got in the boat and went on over to the dock. And when I got over there, Bruce Sloane, who was runnin' the dock, ah, Toby Sloane was

*FIRE IN THE HOLE!*

runnin' the dock, he said, "Big Six, did you have any luck this morning?" I said, "Yeah, we caught a couple of big ones this morning." He said, "What were they?" I said, "Suckers." [43]

Fuzz Anders related the following story about the last time he was 'not caught', which just happened to be by Big Six Henderson and Stanley Groce.

Well, the last time I was not caught. But Big Six and Stanley Groce and them come in here. I lived around here in a little old house around the ridge here. They come in, they come in here...there was another guy that was makin' down below my house down in the holler, and uh, they went down and tore up the place, and they come on around the road after they tore up the place and come on by Ray's and went out the road yonder. And turned around and went back around my house and got a half-gallon jar out of my house, and took it to Cincinnati, Ohio and got my fingerprint off there.[44]

Later in the same interview the subject of Anders' last brush with Big Six was again broached by the interviewer, to which Anders replied:

Well, I just don't remember that. When uh, Big Six and Stanley Groce and, uh, this other revenue man named Bobby come in that time and

52

*FIRE IN THE HOLE!*

run around my house and got that half-gallon jar, I just don't remember what year it was. Two weeks later Big Six come in and picked me up. I'd been hoein' sweet potatoes out 'chear in the garden. And I's layin' under an oak tree. And here come Bobby, Big Six and Stanley Groce. They went to pass by and seen me layin' under that oak tree, and Big Six backed back and jumped outta the car, come down there and says, "Fuzz" says, "I got a warrant for ya." "What you mean you got a warrant for me fer?" He said, "I got a half a gallon jar up from that moonshine still, the worm down there, in Cincinnati, Ohio and got your fingerprints off of it." I said, "Now, Big Six, let me tell you somethin' nother, I know the way you got a half a gallon jar." I said, "I know just exactly what you done, when you went out the road after Rays, you turned around, and went back around my house and got that half a gallon jar you got in Cincinnati, Ohio, and got my fingerprint off of it." I said, "That's what you done."

Didn't have no liquor in it! I'd been gettin' milk out 'chear at uh, that white lady out thar, miss, uh... And I had my jars warshed, on the table. He just went in and got one of 'em off. Sent that off north to Cincinnati, Ohio and got my fingerprint off of it.[45]

The area certainly did not need to have the moonshine business as a means to crime and violence. Life was much harder back when most of these stories are set, which, in turn, made dispensing of the law a more dangerous endeavor.

W.H. Jones, Cumberland County Sheriff from 1913 to 1917, recalls a trip he made to pick up a prisoner from Monroe County:

> That colored boy lived over in Monroe County. Henry K. Maxey; he was out in Zeketown one Sunday and killed one of them Zeke niggers out there. I was over at Mrs. Williams', Gee and I were. We lived at town, but we was over there that Sunday. They had a gab line, talked to the neighbors. Charlie Young lived up where Jim Ed Cary lived. He had a line on long distance, and Mrs. Young could talk to Mrs. Williams on that gab line, and they was trying to get in touch with me some way, to tell me about the murder. They called Mrs. Young, and she called Mrs. Williams about the boy getting killed out there, and to come down and get that nigger. It was getting way down near sundown then, and I called Mrs. Young back and told her to call Milt Smith to meet me at Black's Ferry as soon as he could get there. She got Milt and she could connect us some way. Anyway, I got Milt, but Mrs. Young had to connect us, and she got Milt and I told him to meet me at Black's Ferry.

*FIRE IN THE HOLE!*

I went down there, and Marvin Brewington was the magistrate, and everybody I passed going down there was out in the yard or on the porch to tell me to watch him; he was a mean nigger, and to watch him, that he would kill you if you wasn't careful. That got me sort of shy of him.

I went on down to Marvin Brewington's. He was the magistrate, and I got the warrant for him. He issued warrants, and I got it, and Milt had never got there. I said, "Marvin, why don't you go over there with me to get him?", and he agreed to go, and it was awful hot. I had on a brand new suit of clothes. We went on down to Black's Ferry and hitched our horses, and went across at Cook's, down there at Black's Ferry.

He set us over in that boat. It was narrow, but awful long. I called Mr. Murphy on the gab line from over there at Marvin Brewington's place. Wesley had to come to go with us. We went over there and got him. We had to bring him to the river on the Monroe County line. When he crossed the river, he was in my territory, then I could handle it. When we got down there to the river, he was drunk, singing an old foolish song, cussing with every breath, and when he got down to the edge of the river, he said he would never see the other side of the river. I hadn't never seen that nigger, and I told him, "I don't know you; I never seen you before. I'm going to put these handcuffs on you." He said he was go-

FIRE IN THE HOLE!

ing to turn the boat over, and I said, 'If you turn the boat over, you will never get out with these handcuffs on."

I handcuffed him, and we led him in the boat, and I told him to sit down, and he just stood there and sung. I told him the second time to sit down, and he still just stood there. I had a little .32 pistol about that long, and I stuck that up under his chin, and I told him to sit down. He turned around and finally sat down, but he didn't fall down like I would have.

Marvin Brewington had on a coat, and I did, too. It was hot weather. I don't know how come we were wearing a coat; ordinarily, I would have been in my shirt sleeves. It was way in the night, and he kept singing a foolish song crossing the river, and swearing he was going to turn the boat over. I was standing right behind him, and I was going to knock him in the head if he had started rocking the boat.

Marvin Brewington said he couldn't swim a lick, and he started to pull off his coat and shoes. I said, "What in the hell are you pulling your coat and shoes off, if you can't swim for?" He said he would have a little better chance.

We finally got over there to the ferry boat, and he wanted to sit up on the banisters, and I was afraid he would fall backward in the river. I

*FIRE IN THE HOLE!*

wouldn't let him get up on the banisters. We had to wait a little while. The deputy over there had the gun he killed the nigger with, and we had to have it, you know, and Cook had to go back and get the gun. We had to wait until the ferry boat came back. We got him up on the river bank to our horses. I was sort of afraid to ride in the saddle, and put him up behind me. He could have put his hands over my head, and rolled off with me, and whipped me if he had wanted to. He was a great big nigger. I got my gun out of my saddle, and put it in my front pocket, but still he could have took that away from me, you know. Anyway, I got him up in the saddle, and I got up behind him.

When I got up to Uncle Moses', the sweat was coming through my britches, and I knew I was ruining my suit of clothes. Anyway, we got him off in the yard at old Uncle Mose Cary's out in the wood yard. Marvin Brewington's wife fainted, and he had to go in the house. Directly, I walked to the door and asked if I could be of any help, and Marvin said, "No, I think she is getting better."

I went out and got up in the saddle and got him up behind me. Got way on up the bottom, and I heard someone talking behind me. I guess it was two or three o'clock in the morning. I knowed it couldn't be nobody but Milt, but I couldn't imagine who he was talking to. There was a darkie that lived up the holler, way off the road, and he said, "I have made a many a track up there, but I may never make another one." I said, "I wouldn't be a damned bit surprised if you never make another track on up there." I heard them a talking, and that sort of geared me up a little. They finally overtook us, way up at the far end of the bluff.

I carried him plumb on to Mr. Williams' place, here at Leslie, and I stopped there and got another horse and put that one up. The one I had, had done got tired. I got him up behind me again and come on down here, you know where John Stockton built that new house. The road there went way down the branch to the old Tom Richardson place and around, and we stopped there to get some water. Murley was there and he took him on to town and sure enough they gave him life. After he stayed up there ten or twelve or fifteen years, they turned him out, but he had to go to Indiana and not come back here. They did that a lot back then. They had to leave the state, you know.[46]

This seems to be a recurring act of the courts during this period. Many people were forced to leave their homesteads and find refuge elsewhere when released from prison, or given the option of moving out of state in return for probation.

Not too long ago, that Nell Richardson's husband killed that fellow up there in town, three

*FIRE IN THE HOLE!*

or four years ago. They lived in a trailer on her place somewhere and they fell out about the water or something, and Nell's husband killed this fellow. They put him in prison, but they paroled him in a year or two, but he isn't allowed to come up here and live with Nell. They say Nell goes down there every once in a while.[47]

Mr. Jones tells the following story, reluctantly, about one of his many trips taking prisoners to prison:

I had a bunch of prisoners, two or three, one time, by myself. I rode the train to Louisville, and I got up there, I think about six o'clock. I got off the train, and the jail then was about seven blocks from the depot, and I had to cross the street. I always took my prisoners across Tenth Street, and got over to the other side, and walked on down to the jail. We was always tired and wore out from riding, so we walked that seven blocks.

We got out middle ways of the street, and there was Otis. Otis and his wife had separated, and she was over in Indiana somewhere, and I don't know what Otis was doing up there, but he was pretty drunk, and somebody laid his arm around my shoulder, and it scared me to death for a second until I seen it was Otis.

He went with me and said he was going to go to Frankfort with me. I told him he could go, but

59

he had to sober up. He said he wouldn't drink a drop. We walked on down to the jail, and put our prisoners in the jail. I finally got him to bed that night, way in the night, and we slept to getting up time.

I told him, "Now Otis, if you want to go to Frankfort with me, you can't drink anymore." I said I didn't want him drinking. I said it wouldn't do. He swore he wouldn't drink a drop, and I knew he didn't have none.

We got there at the jail, and got our prisoners, and the first restaurant we passed, I went in and give the prisoners their breakfast. Me and Otis was setting there and I never missed him at all, and he got a pint of liquor some way. I don't know how on earth he got it. We went on down and got on the train, and went on to Frankfort.

Every corner had a mailbox, you know, and he would say, "Let's send one." Back then, there was a lot of postcards with little pictures on them. Before I got him in bed that night, I bet he sent his wife fifty postcards. Every mailbox we got to, he would set down and address his wife one.

So we got on to Frankfort. You could tell he was drinking some. We went on down there to the prison. When we got on down there, he wanted to go in. We could turn them loose there at the gate if we wanted to, but he wanted to go in. I had carried a fellow up there by the name of Henry K. Maxey that had killed one of them Coe niggers one Sunday. They sent him up there for life. There was three big boys sitting there, side by side. He was one of them. I reckon he watched the gate pretty close. Every time I went in, he would throw his hand up at me. I wasn't supposed too talk to him, but I would always say something to him.

Anyway, Otis and myself and the guard went in, all the way around through it. There was a fellow in there, Bill Short, he was in there for life. He had killed two or three down on Pea Ridge. Otis wanted to talk to him. I didn't even want to see him, but Otis did. The guard sent and got him, and Otis talked to him a little while. I had to call Otis my deputy to get him in. The guard said, "Isn't your deputy getting too much wine?" Of course, I was ashamed of him, but I couldn't help it.

We finally got on back to Louisville that night, and we had to leave Louisville at two o'clock. I was afraid to go to bed. I was afraid I wouldn't wake up at two o'clock. We waited around there until two o'clock, and I was afraid the police was going to get him. He was getting pretty drunk. We went on down to the depot, and I got a sleeper to the Glasgow Junction. We got in the bed probably at two o'clock. He had to have the top

61

berth, and I liked not to have got him up in the top berth. I finally got him in the top berth, and I got the one down under him. He rolled out of bed and he busted the floor. I liked not to have gotten him back up there.

We got down to the junction...and there was a colored man there. He came to tell us to get our clothes on. We would be there soon. Of course, I jumped up to put mine on as quick as I could. I helped him get his on. Then, he was getting pretty well sober.

When we got down to the Glasgow Junction, we got off and got on another train and went on to Glasgow, about ten miles. Every once in a while, he would say, "Will, is these my clothes?" I would say, "I don't know; I reckon they are." He'd say, "Will, is these my shoes?" I'd say, "I reckon. I don't know." Of course, he had on a tailor made suit, and it had his name on the inside of the coat pocket. Anyway, he had put on another man's clothes, shoes and all, and this fellow lived down in the western part of the state somewhere, and he found Otis' name in the pocket there, and he wrote Otis, and they changed their clothes through the mail.

Otis had a horse and buggy in Glasgow, and I did too. I started and he followed. Got way out of Glasgow, about ten or twelve miles, and he met some fellow he knew that wanted to sell his

*FIRE IN THE HOLE!*

jack, and he turned back to go buy that jack, and I come on. I don't know whatever happened. I was cramped all the way that time, coming back.

He was pretty drunk, but if he hadn't been with me, they would have arrested him. I was ashamed of him, but I couldn't help it.[48]

When asked if he remembered ever hearing anything about a Joe Coleman, Mr. Jones answered:

I have heard a lot about it and I have heard the song all my life about Joe Coleman. 'Joe Coleman killed his wife, cut her throat with a butcher knife'. I have just heard other people sing it. I heard them say they loaded him on a two-wheeled cart pulled by a yoke of oxen and he rode on his coffin to the hanging place down on the corner next to the old Jim Keen place. Do you know where Albert Stalcup built that new house? They said, he sat on his coffin and played the fiddle or picked the banjo or guitar or something, and he sung the song sitting on his coffin. I just heard about the hanging. He must have felt pretty good sitting on his coffin playing his fiddle.[49]

Although Mr. Jones doesn't seem to know much about the legend of Joe Coleman, there is ample evidence elsewhere that gives weight to the story of the condemned fiddler. According to a Burkesville, Kentucky newspaper publication, The Herald Almanac of 1899...

Joe Coleman, the only white man ever hanged in the county, was hanged, Tuesday, May 25, 1847. He was tried and convicted at the April term of the Circuit Court and the verdict rendered, Saturday, April 17.

He was hanged for killing his wife. The evidence was circumstantial. His wife went to the woods to get some bark, after she had gone he took his shoe knife - he was a shoemaker - and went to the woods also, as he said, to cut a "rock". He came in after a while with her in his arms, dead, and claimed that he had found here dead and murdered. The shoe-knife was found close to the place of the tragedy with blood stains on it. Upon this and other evidence purely circumstantial he was convicted. His wife's sister lived with them at the time and she was the main witness against him. He lived at Slate Fork, Adair County, where his body was taken for burial. Following are the names of the Jurors who tried the case - only one of whom is living - viz: Elisha W. Newby, Jack Lollar, Samuel Brooks, Daniel Swift, John Carter, Pleasant Garrett, George Smith, John Rush, John Fudge, Wm. L. Radford, Irvins Keeton and James Glass. Christopher Tompkins was Judge of this Circuit at that time. Albert G. Waggener was Sheriff and

Milton King, Clerk.

Coleman was granted a change of venue from Adair to Cumberland County. A full jury could not be gotten in this county and part of them were from Clinton. Coleman was hanged on the hill just below the residence of Judge J.J. Simpson. He was driven from the jail - which was the same building in which Sandidge's law office is now located - on a two wheel ox-cart and sat upon his coffin and played "Coleman's March" on the violin as he was taken to the gallows. Jack Doherty, a negro, and father of Jim Doherty, of White's Bottom, drove the cart and was paid $5.00 for same. There was no scaffold and the rope was adjusted and the cart driven from under him and left him dangling in the air. Albert G. Waggener, Deputy Sheriff, tied the rope. He met death without a tremor and plead innocence to the last. James Martin made the gallows and Jack Canady made his coffin in the house in which L.W. McGee now lives. Tommie Low beat the drum and Evans Shaw played the fife.

Years before the hanging of Coleman, Old Peter, a negro slave, was hanged. He was hanged about 250 yards from the place Coleman met his death. He had killed a white woman. He lived on Marrowbone. There are several superstitious stories connected with Old Peter's hanging.[50]

*FIRE IN THE HOLE!*

Mr. Randolph Smith, noted local historian, collected the following story regarding Coleman. The only footnote Mr. Smith provides concerning his sourse is "Newspaper clipping."

More than fifty years ago Joe Coleman was hanged at Burkesville for the alleged murder of his wife. The murder occurred on the farm now owned by Taylor Robinson in Metcalfe County about two miles from Weed, _____ from the testimony _____ of the trial, it appears that Mrs. Coleman was in poor health and wanted a certain bark to make some tea. She told her husband to get it for her and went with him to the woods. Coleman, who was a shoemaker, picked up a shoe knife and carried it along to peel the bark. After they had been gone some time, he returned to the house and asked his sister-in-law where his wife was, saying that after he had gotten the bark for her she had started back to the house. He then asked his sister-in-law to assist him in finding her, and they started out together, Coleman taking the lead. They had not been out long before they came upon the body of Mrs. Coleman lying at the foot of a sapling, cold in death. Her head had been tied to the sapling by her hair and her throat cut from ear to ear. Coleman picked up the body and carried it to the house and the neighbors were notified of the terrible crime. Suspicion seemed to fasten on Coleman from the start and he was arrested for the murder and carried to Burkesville for trial.

He stoutly protested his innocence but the evidence was strong enough to warrant his conviction and the jury found a verdict accordingly.

He was sentenced to hang and the gallows were erected just above the old tan yard within the incorporate limits of Burkesville. When the day of execution arrived a cart containing the condemned man's coffin was driven to the jail door and Coleman took his seat thereon. A few days before, Coleman had asked that two fiddlers be allowed to play "Coleman's March," as the cart and escort proceeded to the place of execution. Bob Higginbottom and Lewis Irvin walked in front of the cart with their violins, playing the march. Arriving at the gallows the rope was adjusted around Coleman's neck, the cart driven away and the doomed man slowly strangled to death. Of Higginbottom and Irvin, the former died in Cumberland County in 1891 and the latter died in _____ in 1904.

The body of the unfortunate Coleman has long since passed to dust and the history of the crime of which he was charged, and his execution is only recalled by the dying statement of a woman in one of the western states, to the effect that she killed Mrs. Coleman. The notice of her death and her confession appeared in a western newspaper and was read by Dr. Cartwright, of Burkesville. We are not informed of the woman's name or the state in which she died.[51]

The facts of this case will forever remain a mystery. Did Coleman kill his wife? Who is the mystery woman that gave the death-bed confession? And did Coleman himself play the fiddle on the way to the gallows? History does show us that there are many folk stories from around the world concerning fiddlers playing while being carted to their ultimate place of execution.

There was a time in the not-so-distant past when a person could be jailed for co-habitating with someone of a different race or color. The white women of Coe Ridge were not spared this indignity when judgement was handed down in this matter.

> I was down there hundreds of times. They always treated me just as nice as could be. I have eat dinner with two or three families down there. There was a few white women down there and they indicted them for living together. Judy Jane Scott, Laura Ellis and Cilla Long was the white women. They lived with Thee Anders, Garfield Wilburn and Cal Coe. Cilla Long lived with Garfield Wilburn, and Laura Ellis lived with Thee Anders, and that Scott woman lived with Cal Coe.
>
> The jury indicted them and sentenced them 500 days in jail each. John Coe come up there and said one of them, Cilla Long, had T.B. Judge Carter made an order and told us to take her to the doctor and if she had T.B., not to bring her.

If the others were able, bring them.

I got a two-seated surrey and me and Oscar went down there. Took us till dinner to get down there. (Oscar Keen)... he was a doctor. When we got down there, they were all out there at Garfield Wilburn's. They invited me and Oscar in to dinner. They said for me and Oscar to eat first and then they would eat. After we ate, Oscar examined Cilla Long and give me an order that she had T.B., so I took the other two women and I brought them to jail. They both died in jail. No, they turned one out just before she died and she went to the hill where she died. Cilla Long didn't die for ten or fifteen years after that. I don't know if she had T.B. or not. All I know is what Oscar said. Garfield Wilburn died and she lived by herself.

(Speaking of Fannie Jo Skipworth) They lived on Potter Creek, just south of Gaines' Hill; that's about a mile. Coe Town is way down in the south end of the county. Them Coe darkies would come up there at Uncle Tom Skipworths and pick the banjo and fiddle. When I was sheriff, old Uncle Cal would preach every night after supper while he was in jail; you could hear him all over town. Jailed him for living with them women. You know, they gave them all 500 days in jail; men and women, too.

They had a hall where the cells were and they

let him out in the hall and old Cal would stand before them iron bars and preach every night. Just about every night he would preach and he could do pretty good, too. Dad was county judge and he bought a Bible and give it to him. I was down there one day, and I think I rode up to his house and he was sitting there reading the Bible and I went on in. And he said, "Your Daddy got me this Bible while I was in jail." I guess, this was years after that.

He said they almost had dinner ready, said they had a quart of mustard cooking. Him and some girl was cooking that mustard. He said it was dinner time and to eat with them, and I did. Cal told me to sit down and eat first. I told him to sit down and eat too. The girl wouldn't, but Uncle Cal sat down and ate. They just had mustard, coffee and corn bread, but it was good.

They didn't have a house fit to live in, but it was clean. One room with a little shed room on one side for cooking.[52]

Fuzzy Anders, speaking of a time when his mother and father were jailed for living together, told the interviewer that his mother was Laura Ellis and his father was Thee Anders. Regarding the fact that they both were incarcerated at one time for living together he said,

"Well, my momma was a white woman and my

*FIRE IN THE HOLE!*

daddy was a colored man, that's the reason, that's the reason they was in jail together." He stated that she "lived with Old Man Cal mostly" before marrying his father. Fuzzy states that Cal also got in trouble for living with a white woman, Judy Jane Scott. He went on to name their children; "He got, uh, Sarah livin', Arthur livin', Loretta livin', and you got another girl named Patsy, she livin'. And he had Cass, and Cordell, and John, they're all dead."

Well, Uncle Cal he stayed five years and five months, and twenty-four days in jail. Well, they come in here and got her (Cal's wife), and she was sick, and they come in here and got her and put her on the horse, and took her and put her in jail and she died in Burkesville jail.[53]

Cold-blooded murder is always a shock when it happens within the confines of a trusted community. It is something that is not supposed to happen in a small, secluded area like Cumberland County, Kentucky. But even here, violence has always been prevalent.

I remember a murder that was inspired by hate or temper. A colored man that lived in our section of the country that worked for a white family, lived with them, was murdered by three brothers who seemed to have some grudge at him about something. I don't know what.

71

The murdered man was a good citizen as far as I knew, but these three brothers and he one day were at a mill in our community that was built up on high pillars and they were under this mill, under this building. And they decided to kill this man. And one of them had a razor.

Those three were Allens, the three brothers, and this man they murdered was a Smith. One of them held him while the others...two of them held him while the others pulled his head back and cut his throat, with a razor, and he thought that the one was named Dent that cut him so. On his death bed statement, he stated that it was Dent but it wasn't Dent, it was his brother. He had taken the razor from his brother Dent and cut the man's throat, so Dent was sent to prison and in the meantime after they cut this man's throat some one came for my father who lived close by to go see if they could do something for him, he was bleeding to death.

Papa had the courage to go there while those men that did the murder were standing around and try to do something for the man but it was to late. He put some spider webs on the cut, which was suppose to stop bleeding but it was to late, and one of these men that was included in the murder got on his bicycle and rode to a church house of colored people while they were having services and he had this blood on his clothing.

*FIRE IN THE HOLE!*

I believe that they let the one that really murdered him go free, he was named Sam and one of the brothers was named Neal. I believe they sent Neal to prison and maybe they sent Dent for life and the real murdered was let go free, because they didn't know that he was the one who did it.[54]

Even when the cause of death was not so premeditated, the ultimate outcome is the same, and the shock is no less...

One murder and robbery was done when I was about 9 years old, close to the time that this black man was killed. We lived at Leslie, maybe 6 or 7 miles from Burkesville, Kentucky and this man that was murdered lived out in the Waterview community. He was married, had a grown son, who was married and some boys decided that they would entice the old man so they wrote letters to him and signed a girl's name of our community to the letters and they got to the point where they wrote a letter to this man to come meet her at a farm out above Burkesville.

In the meantime his wife and daughter-in-law got this letter in the mail and they unsealed it and read the letter and sealed it back and didn't let her husband know that she had read the letter. But she knew her husband was fixing to leave on his horse, and of course she surmised that he was going to meet this girl and she

*FIRE IN THE HOLE!*

begged him not to go but he said, he called her Lina, he says "Now you just as well shut up Lina cause I'm going."

And in this letter this supposed girl had instructed this man to bring all of his money with him, so I don't know if he took all of his money with him, but he went to this farm in the night, and there were 3 boys. It was talked in the neighborhood that they were the 3 that met this man at this place and one of them was dressed in his sisters clothes a posing as this girl.

We thought probably they didn't mean to kill the man but maybe he recognized them and scared them and they shot him. And if I remember rightly he was robbed but we don't know how much money they got, but they didn't take his watch, they left his watch. One of the boys that was supposed to have been in this act had made, or was making, a doctor. So this man was laid out and his eyes were closed, so it must have taken a person who had the experience of working with dead people to have done such a thing.

Nobody was prosecuted for the murder, had no witnesses. One boy, one of the young men was jailed. Put in jail for one night, but not one was prosecuted. The way they found him, his horse was grazing around the next morning in this field, and some one went there and found the body.[55]

FIRE IN THE HOLE!

Marvin Lee remembers his father serving in law enforcement in Cumberland County. A stint as sheriff, as jailer, and as a city policeman were some of the jobs that Mr. Lee held through the years.

> He'd go and travel by horseback then. And ah, he'd be gone for two or three days at a time, days and nights tryin' to catch fellows. And I remember one time in particular he came in. It was real cold weather. Where he had been riding his horse through the creeks, water splashing up on his stirrups, his feet were froze to the stirrups and I had to take a hammer and knock his feet loose from the stirrup, so he could get off his horse.[56]

When asked if his father ever had to use his gun in the line of duty, Mr. Lee stated:

> He, ah, tried to arrest a fellow and he started shooting at daddy. And ah, daddy had to shoot back and wounded the guy and arrested him. And that's about the only time I remember he had to use his gun. He'd go out, even in cold winter weather and lay out sometimes all night, waitin' tryin' to catch moonshiners. Somebody that was wanted for a crime. He would get a tip maybe that they were gonna be at a certain place. Ah, a certain night and he would lay maybe all night long sometimes on a cold frozen ground a waitin' to for the guy to come in. Well,

*FIRE IN THE HOLE!*

he captured and destroyed several moonshine stills and arrested several moonshiners.[57]

Mr. Lee then told the story about his father traveling a long distance in search of a local murderer:

> There was one, one instance a fellow killed another guy in a corn field over, I believe it was on Bear Creek. And the fellow that he killed, his name was Lee. And ah, after he killed the guy he left the state. And ah, of course, daddy began trying to locate him. And it was, for months, months. And he finally got a tip that he was in ah, some other state. I forget what state it was.
>
> But anyway he went after him. And ah, found out where he was staying. And he was staying upstairs in a room. And the, the guy thought that the fellow, he was related to my daddy being named Lee. And he just thought that if daddy ever caught up with him, he just kill him, shoot him down.
>
> So daddy started up the steps where he was staying. Why, he come out the door and started down the steps and when he seen daddy he just throwed up his hands and he begged him not to shoot him. And so of course he didn't have to and he brought him on back and tried him for murder and they sent him to the pen for several years.[58]

Violence was a way of life for a lot of people in this part of the country.

> I had my granddaddy, he killed a fellow, you know, and he got killed. They fight, you know, with knives and they cut one another all to pieces. My granddad got cut 21 times, he cut the other fellows stomach clean across open. And they lived several days. I forgot how many days. And they asked each other, they asked somebody about the other one. If he was still livin' and all like that any, and my granddaddy, he died first.
>
> ...This fellow my granddaddy killed, name was Ed Brown, and a he'd slapped one of his boys, Uncle Job. Slapped him and he come up to granddaddy and told him says, "I had to slap your boy." And my granddaddy, he was drinking heavy you know. And he got his knife and just made him mad, you know, all at once. Just cut his stomach wide open. He had hold his insides in while he opens his knife, his teeth. I mean he opened his knife with his teeth. And he cut my granddaddy then twenty-one times.[59]

When a person was seriously hurt, their fate was usually sealed by the remoteness of the region. Doctors were few and far between, and the slow modes of transportation meant that the injured would probably not make the trip to a distant hospital.

77

Well now, back in them day, when they got shot, back in the day, there wudn't no hospitals around here nowhere. No takin' to Louisville or Nashville, and the family didn't have no money to send 'em there, if they got, bad...you know, shot, bad...cut, that was all of it. They just died. I had a brother-in-law got stabbed in the stomach and Dr. Boles down here at Celina, I mean, Monroe County down here, we went down there and got him and he come to see my brother-in-law and uh, he told my daddy, said, "Thee," says, "If we had him to Nashville ...we could save him." He's a dead man now. That's all it took. He died.[60]

And of course if we are speaking of violent crime and murder, the story of the feud between the residents of Coe Ridge and the Taylor family cannot be overlooked. There are different versions of what happened between these two families. The author will not proceed into conjecture as to the cause of the feud, but will continue in the same fashion as has been previously established. Fuzz Anders relates part of the history of the fued as he heard it.

Well I don't know anything, just what he told me. There used to be a preacher come from Glasgow over here named Preacher Page? He's comin' over about ever summer. And he sat and talked to old man Cal 'bout what happened on this ridge you know, them days? Back in them old days. Well Uncle, he'd set there and tell him all about it you know? You know, how the trou-

78

ble started up in here and all that stuff.

What he told me, and what I heared him told that preacher. That's what the preacher wanted him to tell him you know? It all happened. He said the Taylors come in here you know and just wanted to take over, and run 'em off of'n this ridge.

He told me, that was out 'chear at _____ Water, where the election was out there you know. Where they voted at. And he said they went out there to the election house, and he said he was settin' down, pickin' his old banjo, and he said George Taylor slipped up behind him and shot him in the head, you know the bullet glanced his head, and said his brother, his brother was named Yellow John, and this other John was named Slick John, and said they heared the gunfire. And said they knowed what happened. And George (Taylor) seen 'em a comin', he broke to run and they went to firin' on 'im. And he said his brother run up and hit him across the head with a winchester and bent the barrel on it. And he said Old Man Cal was layin' there said he walked up and kicked Old Man Cal, said his brother John did. Said "Get up Cal! You ain't hurt!" Then Cal got up, and the bullet just glanced his head, and said all them other fellas around there come up and said "Come to see how Cal, see is he hurt?" Said Old Man John Coe, Slick John said, "Everybody walk up one at

*FIRE IN THE HOLE!*

the time", said "walk up one at a time" (to view the the dead man). And that's what he told me, the way that it happened.

That started it. After that they killed Will (Taylor).

Will and Charlie Short and uh, he was a Pruitt, come down there and ask Uncle Cal's mamma says, "Where's Cal at?" She said, "In the back yonder room". Said, "He ain't feelin' good today." They said, "Tell him to git up, we want to see 'im." She went in there and got Old Man Cal up and he went out there and they told Uncle Cal, said, "Hear you had a yoke of steers you want to sell." He said "No, I don't care nothin' 'bout sellin' 'em because...what we got to log with." Then they said, "We want sumthin' to eat." Said , "We hungry." You know, Cal's mamma said to "go over to Aunt Patsy and borrow some meal or flour one. Maybe I cook 'em somethin' to eat." Now he started and..." We just go with ya." Said got up there on the edge of the wood, and Will come out the saddle pack with a quart of liquor and said, "You want a drink uncle?" Said Cal said, "Naw", said "I don't hardly ever drink any much." Said, "Aw, take one." Uncle said he took a little drink, said, "I'll take a shot with ya and show our friendship." When he put that back in there, back in the saddle pack, come out with a big 45. said, "You're the yoke of steers we's lookin' fer." Right there where the trouble started. Told Uncle Cal said, "Call up your crew." Now Cal he commenced to hollerin', makin' some kind of sign you know. And here they come.[61]

Mr. Anders ends his statement at that point, and it seemed that he felt guilt, and hesitance, when talking about the times of the fued with the Taylors. According to Montell's Saga of Coe Ridge, Taylor had told Cal to call up his crew so that he could "wipe them all out." It appears that Taylor was going to shoot Cal when someone hit his arm making the bullet miss its mark.

> I thought he was going to quit, but he began fighting me again. Charlie Short ran from the fence and began to shoot. He shot Oleson Wilburn, but not seriously, and another bullet went through my mother's hair. I started for Short, but saw Taylor aim his gun at me. I grabbed him. I knowed he aimed to kill me for I turned him loose three times and he would start fighting me again. I took my knife and cut his throat.[62]

The entire feuding episode with the Taylors lasted for years. Much information regarding this period of Coe Ridge can be found in Montell's Saga of Coe Ridge and in Chronicles of the Coe Colony by Samuel L. Coe.

Crimes committed locally weren't the only ones that affected those from Cumberland County. One past resident of Cumberland County, Mr. Wilson McComas, spoke of his work

81

within prisons and prison hospitals throughout the United States.

I was Clinical Director of a large prison hospital in Springfield, Missouri, this was called the Medical Center for Federal Prisoners. Had more than 1,000 inmates, some of them were very well known and dangerous criminals.

Well, one man a most interesting man, was called the Bird Man of Alcatraz, he was in prison for murder. I don't remember the details of his crime but he become fascinated with birds and he built beautiful, ornate cages for birds. And through his employment the prison permitted him to sell some of his work and he bought canaries. And he had hundreds of canaries that he'd sell and he trained them to sing with music from a records that he had. He become quite famous and many newspapermen came to the prison and took his picture and wrote up his history and published his stories and so on, very interesting man. He was an introvert, why he committed the crime, I don't know. He was a perfectly fine, nice man in prison.

Another was a famous ah, shall we say a thief, I have to think a moment before I can remember his name. He was the man at that time supposedly stole more money than anyone in history. He was President of the Consolidated Gas and Electric Company in Chicago. And his name still alludes me, I can't think of it. Anyway he, ah, caused no difficulty in prison but, died in prison, he had quite a long term. Matter of fact I think he was accused of having stealing, having stolen, some two or three hundred million dollars through manipulation of stocks and these big utility companies in Chicago and the Central United States.

Another man, very interesting man, was a war criminal who had, had a literally fantastic career and here again I'm having trouble with names. Just right off I can't remember names. This man was of German descent and his first name was Fritz. And he was accused of, and freely admitted, a number of fantastic international crimes. One of which was, he claimed to have murdered the Lord Kitchener. Lord Kitchener was the man who ran the British Armed Forces in the Boer War in South Africa back in the twenties and thirties. And during the war the soldiers, the British soldiers or the people serving under the British Flag attacked villages and towns as soldiers usually do. But they were accused by this man of having murdered his mother, and as a result of this unfortunate affair, and apparently it was historically correct, that this man's mother was killed during the War by British forces. He spent his life revenging his mother's death against the British. And his first purpose was to kill Lord Kitchener. Kitchener was a Field Commander, Army Commander. And shortly before the World War, Second World War, Lord

Kitchener's ship was torpedoed in the British English Channel. And in the instant melee Kitchener was killed. And this man claims credit for it. Whether or not he did it, I don't know. At least he was not caught or prosecuted. He was in prison because he had decided that since the British were fighting the Russians, that he would be on the Russians side. Anyway that he could oppose the British, he would do, because of the feud over his mother's death. And, so he aligned himself with the Russians and he came to the United States and was involved in series of acts of espionage up in the East against the United States who was allied with England and therefore his enemy in his own eye. And eventually tried and convicted of espionage, and was sentenced to a long term in prison. He eventually died in prison. He was an extremely intelligent man, probably a genius. I would, I would guess his I.Q. would be in the region of 150 or 160. And for reading material, he never read novels or histories. He, for his amusements, he read and worked through complicated advanced literature relating to physics and that facts. And he made many attempts to escape from prison, but was never successful. He was a very interesting person to talk to. I spent quite a bit time talking to his man; and learning about his life, very interesting. Many novels could of been written about him. As a matter of fact some reporters came and interviewed him and wrote extensive articles, newspaper articles about him. And these where printed during the war and I'm not sure when he died, but it was sometime shortly after the war.

There were many other interesting people in these prisons where I worked. Following the assignment at Springfield, Missouri. I was the Chief Medical Officer at the famous prison in Leavenworth, Kansas. And here we had even more famous criminals, many of them from the Capone Gang. Gang in Chicago and people of this elk. All are very interesting people if infamous for their crimes. And became well acquainted with many of them. You couldn't generalize about them, I think. They were all types, some of them were introverted people and you would never guess they would be criminals. And others were very aggressive obviously. The criminal tendency, it depended on something of who they were and how they operated. And some of them were hired killers by the Capone Gang.
Others were people who were running rackets various and sundry kinds, most of them multi-millionaires. They made their money in rackets.

Well, for instance some of these people were the principle figures in controlling the sale of boot-legged whiskey, and beer... The Northeastern United States or in and around Chicago. Most of this was smuggled into the states from Canada but, was a multi-million dollar business. And usually involved the assassination of a dozen or more people that were involved, and these were a small percentage of the whole group who happened to be caught and were sentenced to prison. And usually they, if they committed a crime and were taken into the local courts, they bought their way out and were never convicted and it was only the Federal Government who had enough punch to relieve the sentence of these people. Few that were caught were sentenced to the federal court and put into a federal prison from which they couldn't buy their way out.[63]

# Epilogue

It is important that we, as a people, remember such stories as those you've read in this book. It's also important that these tales get passed down to the next generation. The oral history of a particular region is invaluable for the information it contains. When these stories cease to be told, we will have lost part of our heritage. That is one of the purposes of this small endeavour. To help save our local folklore. Some of the tales may be humorous, while others quite unpleasant, but the reality is that they portray a Cumberland County that was, and of which the younger generation has no knowledge.

As stated in the *Introduction* to this book, the hope is that this will be a part of a much larger work of oral history encompassing many facets of life and people in Cumberland County's past. And even though Mrs. Jewell Thomas and her staff did amazing work with the original project, I'm sure there are many, many more stories to be told. I welcome these stories, to be added to either the overall compilation, or another, larger book on moonshining and crime in general. If you, or someone you know, has stories to tell, write them down and either mail, or e-mail, them to one of the addresses found on the Copyright Page at the front of this book.

Thanks for reading these stories. I appreciate it, not just for myself, and my small effort, but for the storytellers, their families, and the subjects of those tales. Keep the folkstories going. Turn off the television, sit on the porch, and tell your children, and grandchildren, the tales you remember.

# Footnotes

1. Ferry Anderson, Age 82, interview conducted at the home of Mr. Anderson in Leatherwood area of Cumberland County, Kentucky by Gail Hubbach, 3 August 1982.
2. Ibid
3. Illus Vincent, Age 71, interview conducted at Cumberland Valley Manor, in Burkesville, Kentucky by LaDonna Graves, 23 April 1980.
4. Document SC 979, pp. 26 - 27, Peggy Bradley Boaz, 1976, Folklife Archives, Kentucky Building, Western Kentucky University, Bowling Green, Kentucky. "Informant C, interview held in Peytonsburg, Kentucky, 23 February 1974. After the interview, Informant C told that he had a dream that he was apprehended by Big Six the night before he was apprehended."
5. Ibid
6. Luna Scott, Age 59, interview conducted in the kitchen of Mrs. Scott's home by LaDonna Graves, 26 May 1980.
7. Carlas Pitcock, Age 73, interview conducted in Mr. Pitcock's trailer in the Mud Camp Community by Sue Ann Pennycuff, 5 August 1981.
8. W.H. (Will) Jones, Age 89, interview conducted at the home of his granddaughter, Joyce Stover, 20 April 1977.
9. Ibid
10. Keith Brewington, interview conducted in the Judio Community of Cumberland County, Kentucky by Marla Lewis, 21 June 1978.
11. Dr. William Lynwood Montell, Saga of Coe Ridge (hereafter referred to in the footnotes as "Montell"), p. 172. Montell also states (in the footnote of the same page) that at another point in the narration, Poindexter claimed that Cal

*FIRE IN THE HOLE!*

had the whiskey in his saddle bags, and that he paid $1.00.

12. Montell, p. 175

13. Ibid. In footnote.

14. Cumberland County News, August 18, 1960, "Coe Ridge Gained Fame For Hideout of Moonshiners."

15. Joe Creason's Kentucky, p. 68.

16. Manuscript SC 979, Chapter II, Page 16, Peggy Bradley Boaz, 1976, Folklife Archives, Kentucky Building, Western Kentucky University, Bowling Green, Kentucky. William Bernard Henderson, interview held in Bowling Green, Kentucky, 2 October 1973. Officials of the Division of Alcohol and Tobacco in Bowling Green stated that their office had only statewide figures of the moonshine stills confiscated, thus could not verify Henderson's claim nor corroborate the year.

17. Manuscript SC 979, Chapter II, Page 16, Peggy Bradley Boaz, 1976, Folklife Archives, Kentucky Building, Western Kentucky University, Bowling Green, Kentucky. William Bernard Henderson, interview held in Bowling Green, Kentucky, 12 December 1973.

18. Manuscript SC 979, Chapter II, Page 14, Peggy Bradley Boaz, 1976, Folklife Archives, Kentucky Building, Western Kentucky University, Bowling Green, Kentucky. Henderson, 23 September 1973.

19. Ibid

20. Document SC 979, Chapter II, p. 18, Peggy Bradley Boaz, 1976, Folklife Archives, Kentucky Building, Western Kentucky University, Bowling Green, Kentucky. Judge James C. Carter, Jr., interview held in Burkesville, KY, 26 March 1974.

21. Cumberland County News, August 18, 1960, Ibid. Also Montell, p. 176.

*FIRE IN THE HOLE!*

22. Manuscript SC 979, Chapter II, Page 19, Peggy Bradley Boaz, 1976, Folklife Archives, Kentucky Building, Western Kentucky University, Bowling Green, Kentucky. Henderson, 12 December 1973. The episode of Fuzzy Anders running from Big Six on crutches is also found in Montell, p. 182; Esther Kellner, Moonshine: Its History and Folklore, p. 181; a similar tale is found in the D.K. Wilgus Miscellaneous Collection, Western Kentucky University Archive of Folklore and Folklife.

23. Elbert "Fuzzy" Anders, interview conducted at Mr. Anders home on Coe Ridge by Frankie Hickey, 1 June 1979.

24. Emmit Cain, Montell, p.182.

25. Manuscript SC 979, Chapter II, Page 19, Peggy Bradley Boaz, 1976, Folklife Archives, Kentucky Building, Western Kentucky University, Bowling Green, Kentucky. Henderson, 2 October 1973.

26. Elbert "Fuzzy" Anders, interview conducted at Mr. Anders home on Coe Ridge by Frankie Hickey, 1 June 1979.

27. Manuscript SC 979, Chapter II, Page 21, Peggy Bradley Boaz, 1976, Folklife Archives, Kentucky Building, Western Kentucky University, Bowling Green, Kentucky. Maurice Clifton "Doc" Keen, interview held in Burkesville, Kentucky, 26 March 1974. In a 4 October 1973 interview held by Lynwood Montell with Big Six, Montell collected the same tale.

28. Elbert "Fuzzy" Anders, interview conducted at Mr. Anders home on Coe Ridge by Frankie Hickey, 1 June 1979.

29. Cumberland County News, August 18, 1960, "Coe Ridge Gained Fame For Hideout of Moonshiners."

30. Montell, p. 178

31. Henderson, 12 December 1973. Joe Coe's perfect record of moonshining and prison is also in Montell, pp. 185-186,

and Kellner, p. 154. Document SC 979, p. 21, Chapter II, Kentucky Library Archives.

32. William Bernard Henderson, interview held in Burkesville, Kentucky, 4 October 1973. Manuscript SC 979, Page 22, Chapter II, Peggy Bradley Boaz, 1976, Folklife Archives, Kentucky Building, Western Kentucky University, Bowling Green, Kentucky. Montell, p. 176-177.

33. Montell, pp. 176-177. Manuscript SC 979, p. 23, Chapter II, Kentucky Library Archives.

34. Henderson, 4 October 1973. The alarm system was used by moonshiners, "Fire in the hole" is also found in Montell, p. 176; Kellner, p. 176. A variant of concern for alarm systems for moonshiners is also found in Wilma Dykeman, The French Broad, p. 302. Manuscript SC 979, Page 23 and 24, Chapter II, Peggy Bradley Boaz, 1976, Folklife Archives, Kentucky Building, Western Kentucky University, Bowling Green, Kentucky.

35. Elbert "Fuzzy" Anders, interview conducted at Mr. Anders home on Coe Ridge by Frankie Hickey, 1 June 1979.

36. Montell, p. 177

37. Henderson, 4 October 1973. Manuscript SC 979, Page 24, 25 and 26, Chapter II, Peggy Bradley Boaz, 1976, Folklife Archives, Kentucky Building, Western Kentucky University, Bowling Green, Kentucky.

38. Informant B, interview held in Peytonsburg, Kentucky, 23 February 1974. Peggy Bradley Boaz, 1976, Folklife Archives, Kentucky Building, Western Kentucky University, Bowling Green, Kentucky

39. William Bernard Henderson, interview held in Bowling Green, Kentucky, 26 September 1973. Peggy Bradley Boaz, 1976, Folklife Archives, Kentucky Building, Western Kentucky University, Bowling Green, Kentucky

40. Henderson, 2 October 1973. Manuscript SC 979, Page 30, Chapter II, Peggy Bradley Boaz, 1976, Folklife Archives, Kentucky Building, Western Kentucky University, Bowling Green, Kentucky.

41. Henderson, 4 October 1973. Manuscript SC 979, Page 22, Chapter II, Peggy Bradley Boaz, 1976, Folklife Archives, Kentucky Building, Western Kentucky University, Bowling Green, Kentucky.

42. Elbert "Fuzzy" Anders, interview conducted at Mr. Anders home on Coe Ridge by Frankie Hickey, 1 June 1979. The baby's name and the name of the resident has been changed due to the sensitive racial nature of the threat.

43. Manuscript SC 979, Page 22, Chapter II, Peggy Bradley Boaz, 1976, Folklife Archives, Kentucky Building, Western Kentucky University, Bowling Green, Kentucky. William Bernard Henderson, interview held in Bowling Green, Kentucky, 31 January 1974. The narrative of apprehending moonshiners and comparing the moonshiners to fish, specifically "suckers," is also found in Kellner, pp. 193-194.

44. Elbert "Fuzzy" Anders, interview conducted at Mr. Anders home on Coe Ridge by Frankie Hickey, 1 June 1979.

45. Ibid

46. W.H. Jones, 20 April 1977, interviewed at the home of his granddaughter, Joyce Stover, by Ms. Jewell W. Thomas, Cumberland County, Kentucky.

47. Ibid

48. Ibid

49. Ibid

50. The Herald Almanac for 1899. A Manual of General Information Pertaining to Cumberland County: Its Resources, Citizens, etc. etc. The Herald, Burkesville, Kentucky.

51. Randolph Smith, The Hanging of Joe Coleman, newspaper clipping, undetermined source.

52. W.H. Jones, 20 April 1977, interviewed at the home of his granddaughter, Joyce Stover, by Ms. Jewell W. Thomas, Cumberland County, Kentucky.

53. Elbert "Fuzzy" Anders, interview conducted at Mr. Anders home on Coe Ridge by Frankie Hickey, 1 June 1979.

54. Mrs. Robbie Stockton, interview conducted at her home by Marla Lewis, 19 July 1978.

55. Ibid

56. Marvin Lee, interview conducted by Marla Lewis, 27 July 1978.

57. Ibid

58. Ibid

59. Carlas Pitcock, Age 73, interview conducted in Mr. Pitcock's trailer in the Mud Camp Community by Sue Ann Pennycuff, 5 August 1981.

60. Elbert "Fuzzy" Anders, interview conducted at Mr. Anders home on Coe Ridge by Frankie Hickey, 1 June 1979.

61. Ibid

62. Montell, p. 98

63. Wilson McComas, interview conducted at the Cumberland County Library by LaDonna Graves, 1 May 1980.

# Index

*FIRE IN THE HOLE!*

# C

*FIRE IN THE HOLE!*

*FIRE IN THE HOLE!*

## L

## M

## N

*FIRE IN THE HOLE!*

*FIRE IN THE HOLE!*

W
Waggener, Albert G.  61
Washington, D.C.  26
Wells, J.W.  24
White, Dave  16
White's Bottom  61
Wilburn
    Bully  41
    Garfield  64, 65
    Oleson  77
Williams, Isom  25, 26, 29, 30, 45, 46

Y
Young, Charlie  51

Z

Zeketown  51

*FIRE IN THE HOLE!*

www.ingramcontent.com/pod-product-compliance
Lightning Source LLC
Chambersburg PA
CBHW062008040426
42447CB00010B/1967